RECIPES FOR HEALTHY LIVING

FORT MYERS CHIP CHAPTER RECIPES

2019 Revised Edition

Typed & Assembled by Andrew Frinkle

Corrections & Edits by Carol Haynes

Cover Design by MediaStream Press

These recipes have been shared by members and supporters of the local program. When possible, credit has been given to the creators and sources of the recipes. If you see one of your recipes in this book or have copyright concerns, please contact us for credit or takedowns. Credits can be added in subsequent editions.

www.fortmyerschip.com

TABLE OF CONTENTS:

BREAKFAST & BREADS:	**PAGE**
APPLES-N-RICE	8
BAKED APPLES	8
BAKED OATMEAL	9
BLUEBERRY WAFFLE TOPPING	9
BREAKFAST BEANS	10
EMULSIFIED NUT BUTTER	10
FRUIT CRISP	11
GRANOLA – SIMPLE RECIPE	12
GRANOLA – SANDRA'S YUMMY RECIPE	13
MILLET CRUMBLE	14
MILLET PUDDING	14
QUINOA	15
PANCAKES – BUCKWHEAT & FLAX	15
RAW BREAKFAST CEREAL	16
SEVEN GRAIN CEREAL	16
UN-SAUSAGE	17
SCRAMBLED TOFU	18
VANILLA SOY MILK	18

SPREADS & SAUCES:

	PAGE
AGAR CHEESE	20
ALFREDO SAUCE	20
AVOCADO MAYO	21
CASHEW ALFREDO	21
CASHEW DILL DIP	22
CASHEW PIMENTO CHEESE SPREAD	22
CASHEW SAUCE	23
CHICKEN SEASONING (VEGAN)	23
COUNTRY STYLE GRAVY	24
DELIGHTFUL TOFU DILL SPREAD	24
DRIED FRUIT JAM	25
GOOD SEASONS ITALIAN DRESSING	25
HUMMUS	26
PARMESAN CHEESE SUBSTITUTE	26
SUNFLOWER CREAM	27
VEGAN SPINACH DIP	28
WHITE BEAN AND SUN-DRIED TOMATO SPREAD	29

ENTREES & MAIN DISHES: PAGE

BAKED TOFU	31
BEST SEASONED BEANS	31
BLACK BEANS	32
BURGER DELIGHT	33
CARROT DOGS	34
CHICKPEA A LA KING	35
CRUISERS	36
DR. DIEHL'S LASAGNA	37
GARDEN NUT BURGER	38
GRILLED BEAN BURGERS	39
HAYSTACKS	40
LIMA BEANS WITH DILL & ONION	40
MILLET TOMATO LOAF	41
PIZZA	41
SLOPPY JOES	42
THAI CURRY	43
TOFU RICE	44
VEGAN ENCHILADAS	45
VEGAN SPRING ROLLS	46
VEGGIE STIR FRY	47
ZUCCHINI BURGERS	48

SOUPS, SALADS, & SIDES: PAGE

15 BEAN SOUP	50
BAKED POTATOES	50
COLESLAW	51
CRUNCHY SOY CORN SALAD	52
DILLY CARROTS & GREEN BEANS	53
EASY BEAN SALAD	53
GREAT GREENS	54
KALE SOUP	55
LENTIL SOUP	56
QUINOA SALAD	57
ROASTED VEGGIES	58
ROASTED GARLIC	58
SCALLOPED POTATOES	59

DESSERTS & SWEETS: PAGE

APPLE ICING BREAD	61
AMBROSIA SALAD	62
BLUEBERRY PIE	63
CAROB CHIP CANDY	64
CAROB PIE	64
CASHEW MAPLE CRÈME	65
FIVE-MINUTE CAROB CAKE	66
FRUIT SMOOTHIES	66
GRANOLA CRUMB CRUST	67
LEMON PIE	67
OUTRAGEOUS CORN MUFFINS	68
STUFFED MEDJOOL DATES	69
SWEET POTATO SALAD	69

RESOURCES: PAGE

THINGS TO ALWAYS HAVE IN YOUR PANTRY	71
BEST STORE-BOUGHT CEREAL OPTIONS	72
BEST HEALTHY SNACKING OPTIONS	73
COOKING WHOLE GRAINS	74
COOKING BEANS	75
VEGAN SUBSTITUTIONS	76
COOKING MEASUREMENTS	77
CHIPPIN' IT OFF (SONG BY WOODY WRIGHT)	78
HEALTHY LIVING AFFIRMATIONS	79

BREAKFAST & BREADS

RECIPES FOR HEALTHY LIVING

APPLES-N-RICE

Preparation Time: 20 Minutes   *Difficulty: Easy*   *Serves: Four*

INGREDIENTS:
- 2 cups brown rice, cooked
- 1 apple, large, cored, peeled & chopped
- ½ cup apple juice, unsweetened
- 2 tbsp. maple syrup
- 1 tbsp. lemon juice
- ½ tsp. cinnamon

DIRECTIONS:
1. Combine all ingredients in casserole dish.
2. Cover and bake at 350° F for 45 minutes.
3. Serve warm or cold. Can also be served as a light supper.

BAKED APPLES

Preparation Time: 15 Minutes   *Difficulty: Easy*   *Serves: 1 per apple*

INGREDIENTS:
- Apples (1 per serving)

DIRECTIONS:
1. Wash apples.
2. Core if desired, but it isn't necessary.
3. Cook in crock pot on low overnight or cover and bake in oven for 45 minutes at 350° F.
4. Serve warm with whole grains or refrigerate and eat cold. So sweet this way!

HINT: Save the juice that forms on the bottom and thicken with corn starch to make a delicious syrup.

BAKED OATMEAL

Preparation Time: 20 Minutes   *Difficulty: Easy*   *Serves: 3-5*

INGREDIENTS:

- ½ cup blueberries
- 1/3 cup dates, chopped, or 1/3 cup raisins
- 2 cups rolled oats
- 1 tsp. vanilla or maple extract
- 4 cups soy milk

DIRECTIONS:

1. Lightly spray a 9"x 9" glass baking dish.
2. Layer first four ingredients in dish in the order given.
3. Mix vanilla or maple extract into soy milk.
4. Pour soy milk evenly over the dry mixture in baking dish.
5. Cover dish and place in refrigerator overnight or bake right away.
6. Bake at 350° F for one hour.

HINT: In the morning serve hot with additional soy or nut milk or unsweetened applesauce.

BLUEBERRY WAFFLE TOPPING

Preparation Time: 15 Minutes   *Difficulty: Easy*   *Serves: 3-5*

INGREDIENTS:

- 1 can frozen, unsweetened grape or apple juice
- 1 can water
- ½ cup corn starch
- 3 cups frozen (thawed) or fresh blueberries

DIRECTIONS:

1. Blend first 3 ingredients until smooth.
2. Pour into saucepan and simmer until thickened.
3. Remove from heat.
4. Serve over waffles or hot cereal.

BREAKFAST BEANS

Preparation Time: 5 Minutes   *Difficulty: Easy*   *Serves: 3-5*

INGREDIENTS:
- 2 – 16 oz. cans chili beans
- 1 – 16 oz. can kidney beans
- 1 – 16 oz. can diced tomatoes with green chili's

DIRECTIONS:

1. Combine all ingredients.
2. Heat in crockpot on low overnight, or cook on stove.

HINT: Any combination of beans may be used. Rinse beans to remove sodium.

EMULSIFIED NUT BUTTER

Preparation Time: 5 Minutes   *Difficulty: Easy*   *Serves: Topping/Garnish*

INGREDIENTS:
- Water
- Nut butter (almond, cashew, etc...)

DIRECTIONS:

1. Mix equal parts of nut butter and water.
2. Stir together thoroughly.
3. Chill before using.

FRUIT CRISP

Preparation Time: 30 Minutes   *Difficulty: Easy*   *Serves: 8-12*

TOPPING INGREDIENTS:
- 3 ½ cups quick oats
- ¼ cup honey or agave
- 2 tbsp. healthy oil
- 2 tbsp. applesauce
- ½ tsp. sea salt

DIRECTIONS:

1. Mix honey, applesauce, and oil.
2. Blend 1 cup of the oats into coarse flour.
3. Mix oats, oat flour, and salt.
4. Add wet ingredients and mix with fingers until crumbly.

FRUIT MIXTURE INGREDIENTS:
- 8 cups sliced or chopped fruit (use fresh or frozen and thawed/drained fruit)
- 4 tbsp. corn starch
- 1 cup chopped dried fruit
- 2 cups unsweetened fruit juice

DIRECTIONS:

5. Place fruit in 9" x 13" baked dish after spraying it.
6. Blend the corn starch and juice together.
7. Pour over the fruit.
8. Top with the oat topping.
9. Bake at 350° F for 35 minutes or until golden brown.
10. Serve hot or cold.

HINT: Use a mixture of fruits. Can also be a dessert if served with Cashew Maple Crème with Citrus (**See recipe in dessert section**).

GRANOLA – SIMPLE RECIPE

Preparation Time: 15 Minutes, Plus Baking Time   *Difficulty: Easy*   *Serves: 5-8*

DRY INGREDIENTS:

- 3 cups rolled oats
- ½ cup unsweetened coconut
- ½ cup chopped walnuts
- ½ tsp. salt

WET INGREDIENTS:

- ¼ cup honey or agave
- 1/8 cup unsweetened applesauce
- 1/8 cup healthy oil
- 2 tbsp. vanilla or maple extract

DIRECTIONS:

1. Mix dry ingredients together.
2. Stir together wet ingredients separately.
3. Pour wet ingredients over the dry mixture and mix well with hands.
4. Press down flat in an 8" x 8" baking dish or spread out ½ inch or thicker on baking sheet.
5. Bake at 190° F or lowest setting for several hours during the night or during the day (up to 6-8 hours). No need to stir.
6. After cooling, break it apart with spatula.

HINT: Add ½ cup raisins after cooking. Chopped nuts, seeds, or other healthy additions can also be made.

GRANOLA – SANDRA'S YUMMY RECIPE

Preparation Time: 90 Minutes   *Difficulty: Easy*   *Serves: 5-8*

DRY INGREDIENTS:
- 9 cups rolled oats (or substitute up to 2 cups of rolled rye or barley for 2 cups of oats)
- 1-2 cups unsweetened coconut ribbons
- 2/3 – 1 cup sunflower seeds
- 1 – 2 cups chopped almonds

WET INGREDIENTS:
- 2 ripe bananas
- 1 cup pitted dates
- ½ cup water
- 1 tsp. vanilla extract
- 1 ½ tsp. salt.

DIRECTIONS:
1. Mix dry ingredients together.
2. Blend the wet ingredients separately.
3. Pour wet ingredients over the dry mixture and mix well.
4. Spread at about ½" thick on a cookie or baking sheet.
5. Bake at 200° F for 90 minutes, stirring every 30 minutes until golden and almost dry.
6. Turn oven off and leave pans in oven to complete drying.
7. Break granola apart after allowing it to cool. Store in airtight container.

HINTS: For flakier granola, increase by 1 cup of oats. For crunchier, use 1 cup less oats.

MILLET CRUMBLE

Preparation Time: 75 Minutes   *Difficulty: Moderate*   *Serves: 5-8*

INGREDIENTS:
- 1 cup millet
- 3 cups water
- 3 cups unsweetened pineapple juice
- 3 tsp. vanilla
- 1 tsp. salt
- 1 ½ tsp. grated lemon rind.
- 4 cups granola or 2 cups granola and 1 cup unsweetened coconut
- 4 cups sliced bananas (you can substitute blueberries instead)

DIRECTIONS:
1. Bring water to boil in a saucepan.
2. Add millet. Cover and simmer 45-60 minutes.
3. When millet is done, blend the following on high speed until creamy to make millet pudding: 1 cup hot cooked millet, ¾ cup pineapple juice, 1 tsp. vanilla, dash of salt.
4. Place 2 cups granola on bottom of a 9" x 13" baking dish.
5. Layer sliced bananas on top of granola.
6. Pour millet pudding over bananas.
7. Repeat for 2 more layers of pudding and bananas.
8. Top with remaining 2 cups granola or sprinkle the unsweetened coconut on top.
9. Chill uncovered until firm.

HINT: Do not add extra vanilla, or the dish may not set, because of the alcohol content.

MILLET PUDDING

Preparation Time: 10 Minutes   *Difficulty: Easy*   *Serves: 3-5*

INGREDIENTS:
- 1 cup cooked hot millet
- 1 tbsp. honey
- ¾ cup pineapple juice
- 1 tsp vanilla

DIRECTIONS:
1. When millet is done cooking, blend all ingredients on high speed until creamy
2. Chill uncovered until firm.
3. Top with coconut or other garnishes.

PANCAKES – BUCKWHEAT & FLAX

Preparation Time: 10 Minutes   *Difficulty: Easy*   *Serves: 2-4*

INGREDIENTS:
- ¾ cup whole wheat flour
- ½ cup buckwheat flour
- 2 tsp. aluminum free baking powder
- 2 tbsp. pure Florida Crystals sugar or sweetener of your choice.
- 1 tbsp. flax seed
- ½ tsp. cinnamon
- 1 tsp pure vanilla
- 2 tbsp. canola oil
- 1 ¼ cup soy milk

DIRECTIONS:
1. Mix dry ingredients in a small bowl.
2. Slowly add wet ingredients and stir until well mixed.
3. Pour batter in 5" circles on a hot skillet sprayed with non-stick cooking spray.
4. When bubbles appear on top of pancake, flip over with spatula. Brown other side and remove from pan.
5. Serve with your favorite toppings.

HINT: This batter can be used to make waffles, also.

QUINOA

Preparation Time: 5 Minutes   *Difficulty: Easy*   *Serves: 3-5*

INGREDIENTS:
- 1 cup quinoa
- 2 cups water

DIRECTIONS:
1. Rinse quinoa in strainer and drain.
2. Combine quinoa and water in a kettle or pan.
3. Bring to a boil, reduce to a simmer, and cook 10-15 minutes until water is absorbed. Grains should be transparent when cooked.
4. Fluff with a fork.

HINT: Quinoa naturally has a bitter coating to protect it from insects. Most brands rinse this off prior to packaging, but rinsing before eating is a good idea anyway.

RAW BREAKFAST CEREAL

Preparation Time: 15 Minutes   *Difficulty: Easy*   *Serves: 2-4*

INGREDIENTS:
- 1 cup soaked oats groats
- 1 cup soaked almonds or walnuts
- 1/3 cup soaked raisins
- 2 tbsp. pure maple syrup
- 1 tbsp. pure vanilla
- fresh fruit for topping
- non-dairy milk

DIRECTIONS:
1. Process all ingredients in a food processor using an S-blade until ground but chunky.
2. Spoon into cereal bowls and serve with non-dairy milk.
3. Top with fresh kiwi, apples, banana, grapes, or berries.
4. Store in a covered container in refrigerator for up to a week.

HINT: This recipe can also be used as a topping for other hot cereals. The high concentration of nuts will help in a fat-reduction program. Use 2 tbsp. for topping.

SEVEN GRAIN CEREAL

Preparation Time: 5 Minutes   *Difficulty: Easy*   *Serves: 2-3*

INGREDIENTS:
- 1 cup Bob's Red Mill seven grain cereal (brown rice, oats, barley, millet, wheat, corn, quinoa)
- 3-4 cups water
- 1 tbsp. ground flax seed per bowl/serving
- Toppings of your choice

DIRECTIONS:
1. Spray the inside upper edge of a crock pot with non-stick spray.
2. Put cereal in water in the crock pot.
3. Turn crock pot on low, cover, and let cook for 6-8 hours (or overnight).
4. Serve with non-dairy milk and top with fresh ground flax seed.

HINT: You can also top with fresh fruit, dried fruit, raisins, walnuts, or cardamom.

UN-SAUSAGE

Preparation Time: 30 Minutes   *Difficulty: Easy*   *Serves: 4-6*

INGREDIENTS:
- 2 cups quick oats
- 2 cups water
- 3 tbsp. soy sauce
- 2 tsp. honey
- 2 tsp. onion powder
- 2 tbsp. olive oil
- 1 tsp. sage
- ½ tsp. garlic powder
- ½ tsp. Italian seasoning

DIRECTIONS:
1. Combine water and seasonings in saucepan.
2. Bring to a boil. Add oats and cook 1-5 minutes until tender.
3. Spray a cookie sheet. Use a small ice cream scoop and place scoops onto a cookie sheet. Flatten each scoop with the back of a spoon to make round sausage patty shapes.
4. Bake at 350° F for 8-15 minutes on each side.

SCRAMBLED TOFU

Preparation Time: 5 Minutes   *Difficulty: Easy*   *Serves: 2-3*

INGREDIENTS:
- 1 pkg. medium/firm tofu
- ½ tsp. garlic powder
- 1 tsp. onion powder
- ¼ - ½ tsp. turmeric
- ½ tbsp. dried parsley
- ½ tbsp. Bragg's all-purpose seasoning
- 1-3 tsp. chicken-like seasoning of your choice, to taste
- ½ tbsp. nutritional yeast flakes

DIRECTIONS:
1. Preheat a large nonstick frying pan.
2. Drain and rinse tofu. Chop and mash with a spoon and put in frying pan.
3. Sprinkle all seasonings equally over tofu. Mix well.
4. Stir occasionally, cooking until most of the moisture has disappeared.
5. Serve fresh and hot, garnishing with fresh parsley and tomato, or optionally mushrooms and peppers.

VANILLA SOY MILK

Preparation Time: 10-15 Minutes + machine recipe time   *Difficulty: Easy*   *Serves: 4-6*

INGREDIENTS:
- 6 cups water
- ½ cup soaked soy beans
- 2 tbsp. oats
- ¼ tsp. salt
- 1-2 tbsp. honey
- 1 tbsp. vanilla
- 1/8 – ¼ tsp ginger (optional)

DIRECTIONS:
1. Fill soy milk maker to line with water (about 6 cups).
2. Add soybeans and oats and optional ginger, if desired.
3. Start machine.
4. When machine is done, stir honey and vanilla into hot milk.
5. Strain milk through sieve or cheesecloth. Pulp can be used for cooking.

HINTS: You can substitute ¾ cup almonds or cashews soaked overnight for the soy beans. You can also measure out bags of pre-soaked soy beans, keeping them handy in the freezer for when you want to make this recipe. Finally, other grains can be used instead of oats for a thickening agent, but they will have to be soaked prior to use.

SPREADS & SAUCES

RECIPES FOR HEALTHY LIVING

AGAR CHEESE

Preparation Time: 15 Minutes   *Difficulty: Easy*   *Serves: Garnish/Spread*

INGREDIENTS:
- 1 cup water
- 3-4 tbsp. agar flakes
- 2/3 cup raw cashews
- ½ cup water
- 1/3 cup pimentos
- 3 tbsp. yeast flakes
- 2 tbsp. lemon juice
- 2 tsp. onion powder
- 1 ½ tsp. salt
- ½ tsp. garlic powder

DIRECTIONS:

1. Lightly boil agar in 1 cup of water for 3-4 minutes until it is clear. Remove from heat.
2. Blend smooth all remaining ingredients.
3. Pour hot agar into blender, scraping pan with rubber spatula to get all the agar out.
4. Pour in other blended ingredients and blend everything until the same consistency.
5. Pour into a container and chill.

ALFREDO SAUCE

Preparation Time: 5 Minutes   *Difficulty: Easy*   *Serves: 4-6*

INGREDIENTS:
- 1 pkg. firm silken tofu
- ½ cup water or soy milk
- 1 tbsp. extra virgin olive oil
- 1-2 cloves minced garlic or ¼ tsp. garlic powder
- 3 tbsp. nutritional yeast
- 1 tbsp. dried parsley
- 1 tsp. salt
- 1 tsp. onion powder
- 1 tsp. basil

DIRECTIONS:

1. Blend all ingredients together until smooth. Warm to serve.
2. Serve over pasta or other healthy alternative.

AVOCADO MAYO

Preparation Time: 5 Minutes   *Difficulty: Easy*   *Serves: Garnish/Spread*

INGREDIENTS:
- 1 cup pine nuts
- 1 avocado
- 1 tbsp. lemon juice
- 2 tbsp. apple cider vinegar
- 1 tsp. sea salt
- 6 medium pitted dates (makes 3 packed tbsp.)
- 1 clove garlic

DIRECTIONS:

1. Remove skin and pit from avocado.
2. Mix all ingredients until smooth.

HINT: Use as a spread or as a dip.

CASHEW ALFREDO

Preparation Time: 15 Minutes   *Difficulty: Easy*   *Serves: 4-6*

INGREDIENTS:
- ½ cup raw cashews
- 1 ½ cup boiling water
- 1 tsp. fresh lemon juice
- 1-2 cloves minced garlic
- 1 tsp. onion powder
- 2 tbsp. parsley
- ½ cup nutritional yeast
- 1 pkg. silken tofu
- salt and pepper to taste
- ½ cup sun-dried tomatoes or mushrooms (optional)

DIRECTIONS:

1. Process cashews until ground.
2. Carefully add the water and blend for 2 minutes.
3. Add the rest of the ingredients and blend until an even consistency.
4. Add to pasta or favorite recipe.

HINT: Sun-dried tomatoes or mushrooms add nutrition and flavor.

CASHEW DILL DIP

Preparation Time: 15 Minutes   *Difficulty: Easy*   *Serves: Garnish/Spread*

INGREDIENTS:

- 1 cup cashews or sunflower seeds
- 1 cup hot brown rice or millet
- 1 cup water
- 1 tsp. salt
- 2 tsp. onion powder
- ½ tsp. garlic powder
- ½ tsp. dill weed
- ¼ cup lemon juice

DIRECTIONS:

1. Blend all ingredients until smooth, using a spatula as necessary.
2. Serve on baked potatoes, as a veggie/cracked dip, or as a sour cream substitute.

HINT: Added water can also be used to make this a sauce, rather than a dip.

CASHEW PIMENTO CHEESE SPREAD

Preparation Time: 15 Minutes   *Difficulty: Easy*   *Serves: Garnish/Spread*

INGREDIENTS:

- ¾ cup raw cashews
- ¾ cup water (or pimento juice)
- ¾ cup diced pimentos (red peppers)
- ½ cup nutritional yeast flakes
- 1 tsp. salt
- 2 tsp. onion powder
- 1 tsp. garlic powder
- 1/3 cup lemon juice
- ¼ cup quick dry oats

DIRECTIONS:

1. Blend first 4 ingredients until very creamy.
2. Add remaining ingredients and blend until smooth.
3. Pour into saucepan and stir constantly over medium heat until thick. A wire whisk works well for this.

HINT: If you want a thinner sauce, eliminate the oats. You can also omit the cashews and increase the oats to ¾ cup for a fat-free recipe.

CASHEW SAUCE

Preparation Time: 5 Minutes   *Difficulty: Easy*   *Serves: Garnish/Spread*

INGREDIENTS:
- 1 cup cashews
- 1 tsp. salt
- ½ tsp. onion powder
- ¼ tsp. garlic powder
- 2 oz. Pimentos
- 2 tbsp. lemon juice
- 1 cup water

DIRECTIONS:

1. With blender running, add just enough water to process. Whiz until smooth.
2. Add remaining water and mix until even in consistency.

HINT: Added water can also be used to make this a sauce, rather than a dip.

CHICKEN SEASONING

Preparation Time: 5 Minutes   *Difficulty: Easy*   *Serves: Seasoning*

INGREDIENTS:
- 1 1/3 cup nutritional yeast flakes
- 3 tbsp. onion powder
- 2 ½ tsp. garlic powder
- 2 ½ tbsp. sea salt
- ½ tsp celery seed
- 2 tbsp. Italian seasoning
- 1 tbsp. parsley flakes

DIRECTIONS:

1. Blend ingredients until smooth.
2. Store in a glass container to use as flavoring for soups, gravy, patties, etc...

COUNTRY STYLE GRAVY

Preparation Time: 15 Minutes   *Difficulty: Easy*   *Serves: 3-4 with entrée*

INGREDIENTS:

- 2 cups water
- ½ cup cashew pieces
- 1 tbsp. onion powder
- ½ tsp. garlic powder
- 3 tbsp. soy sauce
- 1 tbsp. yeast flakes
- 1 tbsp. corn starch

DIRECTIONS:

1. Blend cashews with 1 cup water until creamy.
2. Add remaining water and other ingredients.
3. Blend until creamy.
4. Pour into saucepan and cook on medium-high until thick, stirring constantly.
5. Serve over entrée, potatoes, or biscuits.

DELIGHTFUL TOFU DILL SPREAD

Preparation Time: 5 Minutes   *Difficulty: Easy*   *Serves: 14x 2 tbsp.*

INGREDIENTS:

- 1 pkg. extra firm silken tofu
- ½ cup vegannaise
- 1 ½ tsp. dill weed
- ½ tsp. onion powder
- ½ tsp. salt
- 1 tsp. dried, minced onion
- 1 tsp. honey or agave

DIRECTIONS:

1. In a medium-sized food processor, process to smooth or blend thoroughly.
2. Transfer to a container and refrigerate until flavors blend.

HINT: This can be used on baked potatoes or as a veggie dip.

DRIED FRUIT JAM

Preparation Time: 5 Minutes   *Difficulty: Easy*   *Serves: Garnish/Spread*

INGREDIENTS:
- 1 cup dried unsweetened apricots
- 1 cup date pieces
- 2 cups pineapple juice

DIRECTIONS:

1. Lightly boil the ingredients in a covered saucepan until the fruit has softened.
2. Mash to make a chunky spread or blend for a smooth spread.

HINT: Vary the juice and/or the fruit for different flavors. Beware of most dried berries, as they may have added sugars. Read labels before buying.

GOOD SEASONS ITALIAN DRESSING

Preparation Time: 5 Minutes   *Difficulty: Easy*   *Serves: Garnish/Spread*

INGREDIENTS:
- 1 pkg. Good Seasons Mix
- ¼ cup lemon or lime juice
- ¼ cup water
- 1 tbsp. olive oil
- ½ cup orange juice with pulp
- 1 tbsp. pure maple syrup

DIRECTIONS:

1. Add seasoning mix to water and lime juice. Cover and shake well.
2. Add oil, juice, and syrup to the mix. Cover and shake well again.
3. Serve immediately, or store in the refrigerator for up to 4 weeks.

HUMMUS

Preparation Time: 5 Minutes   *Difficulty: Easy*   *Serves: Garnish/Spread*

INGREDIENTS:
- 1 can garbanzo beans – drain all but ¼ cup juice
- 2 tbsp. tahini or 1/3 cup avocado
- 2 tsp. onion powder
- 1 tsp. garlic powder or 2 whole cloves of garlic
- ¼ cup lemon juice
- ½ tsp. salt

DIRECTIONS:

1. Blend everything together until creamy.
2. Optionally, stir in black olives, red roasted peppers, or pine nuts for flavor.
3. You can also add 6 artichoke hearts, 3 sliced green onions, or ¼ cup sun dried tomatoes to the blender.

HINT: Experiment with different seasonings, such as cumin, cayenne pepper, or turmeric.

PARMESAN CHEESE SUBSTITUTE

Preparation Time: 5 Minutes   *Difficulty: Easy*   *Serves: Garnish/Spread*

INGREDIENTS:
- 1 cup lightly toasted sesame seeds
- ½ cup yeast flakes
- ½ tsp. onion powder
- ½ tsp. garlic powder
- ½ tsp. salt
- ½ tsp. dried lemon peel

DIRECTIONS:

1. Put all ingredients except yeast flakes into the blender. Blend until the seeds are ground and pulverized.
2. Empty ground materials into a bowl and add yeast flakes. Mix thoroughly.
3. Refrigerate.

SUN CREAM

Preparation Time: 5 Minutes   *Difficulty: Easy*   *Serves: Garnish/Spread*

INGREDIENTS:

- 1 cup raw sunflower seeds
- 1 tsp. salt
- 2 tsp. onion powder
- ¼ tsp. garlic powder
- 1/8 tsp. celery seed (optional)
- 2-4 tbsp. nutritional yeast flakes (optional)
- 1 cup water
- 3 tbsp. lemon juice

DIRECTIONS:

1. Whiz together all dry ingredients until crumbly.
2. Add the water and lemon juice.
3. Whiz together until very smooth.
4. Store in refrigerator.

HINT: This recipe can be used instead of mayo, sour cream, gravy, alfredo, or even as an egg substitute. It can also be used in scalloped potatoes by adding half an onion and a garlic clove to the mixer with the other ingredients.

VEGAN SPINACH DIP

INGREDIENTS:

- 1 cup cashews
- ¾ cup almond milk
- ½ cup canned cannellini beans, rinsed
- 1 tbsp. olive oil
- 1 tbsp. lemon juice
- 1 ½ tsp. Bill's Best Chik'nish Seasoning
- 10 oz. frozen spinach
- ¼ cup minced garlic (about 6 large cloves)
- 1 1/2 – 2 cups chopped onions (about 1 whole)
- 1 tsp olive oil
- ¼ tsp. salt
- ¼ tsp cayenne pepper
- ½ can water chestnuts, chopped (optional)

DIRECTIONS:

1. Blend cashews, almond milk, beans, olive oil, lemon juice, and seasoning together until smooth.
2. Defrost spinach. Squeeze out excess water and chop.
3. Sauté onion and garlic in olive oil. Add garlic later, so it doesn't burn.
4. Add cashew/bean mixture from step 1 to the onions and garlic. Mix well.
5. Mix in the chopped spinach. Cook on medium heat until dip is warm throughout.
6. If you want the dip to be thinner, add water or almond milk until thinned to a consistency you like.
7. Taste. Add seasonings and water chestnuts, if desired.

HINT: For less fat, use ½ cup cashews and 1 cup cannellini beans instead. Also, do step 3 with water instead of oil.

WHITE BEAN SPREAD WITH TOMATO

Preparation Time: 20 Minutes   *Difficulty: Easy*   *Serves: Garnish/Spread*

INGREDIENTS:

- 6 sun-dried tomatoes (not packed in oil)
- 1 cup boiling water
- 1 ½ cups cooked or canned great northern beans, rinsed and drained
- 1 tsp. finely chopped rosemary or 1 tsp. crumbled dry rosemary
- 1 tsp. fresh lemon juice
- 2 cloves garlic, minced or pressed, or ½ tsp. garlic powder
- ½ tsp. salt
- ½ tsp. sage
- ½ cup bean cooking liquid or vegetable broth (optional)

DIRECTIONS:

1. Place tomatoes in heat-safe container and pour boiling water over them. Soak until softened (about 10 minutes).
2. Drain, thinly slice, and set aside.
3. Combine beans, herbs, and other ingredients (other than the tomatoes) and process until smooth. If desired, add the broth or bean liquid at this point to achieve desired texture.
4. Stir in sun-dried tomatoes.
5. Taste and season with more salt or lemon juice, if needed.
6. Store in a container in the refrigerator for up to 3 days.

*Recipe adapted from *The Get Healthy, Go Vegan Cookbook* by Neal Barnard, M.D., and Robyn Webb.

ENTREES & MAIN DISHES

RECIPES FOR HEALTHY LIVING

BAKED TOFU

Preparation Time: 30 Minutes   *Difficulty: Easy*   *Serves: 3-4*

INGREDIENTS:
- ½ cup McKay's Chicken or Beef Seasoning (Vegan and MSG-Free)
- ¾ cup nutritional yeast flakes
- 2 tbsp. onion powder
- 1 tbsp. garlic powder
- 1 tbsp. turmeric
- 1 cup dried parsley or chives
- salt to taste
- 1 – 2 pkgs. firm or extra firm tofu (refrigerated tofu)

DIRECTIONS:
1. Mix or blend all seasonings thoroughly.
2. Slice tofu into ¼ inch slices.
3. Dip slices into seasoning.
4. Lay on sprayed sheet.
5. Bake at 350° F for 15 minutes.
6. Flip slices and bake 10 more minutes, or until slightly browned.

BEST SEASONED BEANS

Preparation Time: 15 Minutes   *Difficulty: Easy*   *Serves: varies*

TYPE OF BEANS:
- Pinto Beans – onion, garlic, basil, cumin, salt
- Lima Beans – onion, dill, salt, olive oil
- Black Beans – onion, garlic, green pepper, cumin, olive oil, oregano, capers, tomato sauce, salt
- Garbanzo Beans – onion, veggie chicken seasoning, garlic, basil, salt
- Lentils – Bay leaf, oregano, tomato sauce, olive oil, salt

SERVING & PREPARATION SUGGESTIONS:
- Always add salt after beans are tender, and eliminate salt if using canned beans.
- Serve beans over your favorite grains.
- Mash beans for homemade burritos, enchiladas, and tacos.
- Create taco salads with beans, chips, and veggies.
- Use beans as a baked potato filler.
- Eat beans with toast for breakfast.

BLACK BEANS

Preparation Time: 20 Minutes   *Difficulty: Easy*   *Serves: 4-6*

INGREDIENTS:
- 2 tbsp. olive oil
- 1 cup finely chopped onion
- ½ cup chopped green pepper
- 4 cloves minced garlic
- 1 can of 1 lb. 13 oz. Goya black beans, undrained
- ½ tsp. crushed oregano leaves
- ½ tsp. chopped capers (optional)
- 4 oz. tomato sauce
- ½ cup water + 1 tbsp.
- 1 tsp. salt, or to taste
- 1 tbsp. green olives

DIRECTIONS:

1. Heat oil in large saucepan over medium heat.
2. Add onion, pepper, garlic, and tomato sauce. Cook until tender (approx. 5 minutes).
3. Stir in remaining ingredients.
4. Reduce heat and simmer 5-10 minutes.
5. Serve over rice or your favorite grain.

BURGER DELIGHT

Preparation Time: 20 Minutes   *Difficulty: Easy*   *Serves: 18x 2/3 cup servings*

INGREDIENTS:

- 2 cups Bulgur Wheat (not fine-ground)
- 4 cups canned tomatoes
- ½ medium onion chopped
- 2 – 3 cloves garlic
- 1 cup walnuts (pecans or raw sunflower seeds can be substituted)
- 2 tsp. salt
- 2 tbsp. molasses

DIRECTIONS:

1. Place the wheat in a saucepan.
2. Blend all other ingredients until smooth.
3. Add blended ingredients to wheat and mix.
4. Simmer for 20 minutes, stirring occasionally.
5. Spread mixture evenly on a sprayed cookie sheet.
6. Bake at 250-275° F for 45-60 minutes, until it is a loose, burger-like consistency.
7. Stir occasionally while baking, not burning it or overcooking it.
8. Remove from oven while it is still moist.

HINT: Serve with potatoes, pasta, or over a whole grain. Burger can also be added to sauces or used in chili.

*Recipe adapted from *Guilt-Free Gourmet* page 22.

CARROT DOGS

Preparation Time: 15-20 Minutes, plus overnight   *Difficulty: Easy*   *Serves: 4*

INGREDIENTS:
- 4 large carrots
- Water to boil carrots
- ¼ cup apple cider vinegar
- ¼ cup water
- 2 tbsp. low-sodium tamari
- 1 tsp. molasses
- ¼ tsp. liquid smoke
- ¼ tsp. garlic powder
- ¼ tsp. onion powder
- ¼ tsp. black pepper
- 4 whole-grain hot dog buns, toasted if desired

DIRECTIONS:

1. Peel and trim carrots. Cut them to bun length.
2. Bring medium saucepan of water to boil over medium-high heat.
3. Add and cook carrots until tender, but not mushy, approximately 5-8 minutes.
4. Drain the carrots in a strainer and run cold water over them to stop cooking.
5. In a small bowl, whisk together the vinegar, water, tamari, molasses, liquid smoke, and other spices.
6. Transfer the marinade to a large Ziploc bag and put the carrots in. Toss gently and refrigerate overnight.
7. Preheat oven to 400° F. Use parchment on a rimmed cooking sheet, and bake 15-20 minutes until heated through and slightly browned.
8. Serve carrots in hot dog buns with your choice of toppings.

HINT: Serve with potatoes, pasta, or over a whole grain. Burger can also be added to sauces or used in chili.

*Recipe adapted from Kim Campbell's *Plantpure Kitchen*

CHICKPEA A LA KING

Preparation Time: 15-20 Minutes   *Difficulty: Moderate*   *Serves: 3-5*

SAUTE INGREDIENTS:
- ½ cup chopped onions
- ½ cup sliced mushrooms
- 1 tbsp. oil
- 2 tbsp. water

BLENDING INGREDIENTS:

- ½ cup cashew pieces
- 1 cup water
- 4 tsp. veggie chicken seasoning
- 1 tsp. garlic powder
- 4 tsp. onion powder
- ¼ cup corn starch
- 1 tbsp. Bragg's Liquid Amino Acid or Soy Sauce
- 2 tbsp. nutritional yeast flakes

FINAL INGREDIENTS:

- 3 cups water or liquid for garbanzo beans
- 2 cups frozen peas (thawed)
- ½ cup chopped pimentos
- 2 cups cooked or canned garbanzo beans

DIRECTIONS:

1. Sauté onions and mushrooms in oil and water until onions are clear. Set aside.
2. Blend cashews with 1 cup of water and next 6 ingredients until very creamy.
3. Boil 3 cups of water.
4. Pour blended mixture into boiling water, stirring until thickened.
5. Add onions, mushrooms, garbanzos, pimentos, and peas.
6. Continue to stir and cook for 2 more minutes.
7. Serve over brown rice, whole grain noodles, or toast.

CRUISERS

Preparation Time: 30 minutes　　　*Difficulty: Easy*　　　*Serves: 6-10 patties*

INGREDIENTS:
- 1 cup frozen peas or mixed veggies (thawed if desired)
- 15 oz. can of tomatoes
- 2 tbsp. soy sauce
- 1 tbsp. onion powder
- ½ tsp. garlic powder
- ¼ tsp. salt
- ½ tbsp. Italian herbs
- 2 tsp. McKay's or Bill's Best Seasoning
- 2 cups quick oats

DIRECTIONS:

1. Blend all ingredients except oats until pureed.
2. Stir oats into puree until even in consistency.
3. Using a spoon or ice cream scoop, place mounds on a sprayed cookie sheet. Flatten them into patties. These can also be made into meatball shapes, but that will reduce the baking time.
4. Bake in oven at 350° F for 20 minutes. Flip and back them 10-15 more minutes. Reduce time by up to 5 minutes per step for smaller patties or meatballs.

HINTS: Good in sandwiches or by themselves. You can also freeze them. Another option is to pan fry them over low heat in a covered, sprayed, non-stick pan.

DR. DIEHL'S LASAGNA

Preparation Time: 30 minutes   *Difficulty: Moderate*   *Serves: 6-8*

INGREDIENTS:

- 8 cups marinara sauce
- 1 lb. ground meatless burger by Morningstar Farms or **Burger Delight Recipe**
- 2 cups dairy-free tomato soup
- 3 tbsp. beef-like seasoning
- 1/3 cup onion flakes
- ½ tsp. garlic powder
- 1 finely-chopped green pepper
- 2 finely-chopped celery stalks
- 1 tsp. Italian seasoning
- 1 lb. whole grain Lasagna Noodles
- 2 pkgs. firm silken tofu
- 1/3 cup chopped parsley

DIRECTIONS:

1. In a medium-sized pot, combine all ingredients except the noodles, tofu, and parsley.
2. Bring to a boil, reduce heat, and simmer for 40 minutes.
3. Place noodles in boiling water and cook until tender, as per package instructions.
4. Layer in a 9" x 13" pan: tomato sauce, noodles, and then tofu. Repeat until all ingredients have been used or until the pan is nearly full.
5. Bake at 350° F for 45 minutes.
6. Garnish with freshly chopped parsley.

HINTS: Sliced mushrooms can be added to this dish. You can also top with vegan cheeses, such as our **Agar Cheese** recipe. You want to add it at the end of the baking, just long enough to get it to melt.

*Recipe adapted from Dr. Hans Diehl

GARDEN NUT BURGERS

Preparation Time: 15-20 minutes   *Difficulty: Easy*   *Serves: 4-8 patties*

INGREDIENTS:

- ½ cup finely-chopped walnuts
- ½ tsp. salt
- 1 tbsp. yeast flakes
- 1 tsp. garlic powder
- 1 tsp. beef-like seasoning
- ½ cup quick oats
- 1 cup soft whole wheat bread crumbs
- ½ cup finely-grated carrots
- 1 finely-chopped medium onion
- 1 tbsp. Bragg's Liquid Amino Acids or soy sauce
- 1 cup soft tofu, drained well

DIRECTIONS:

1. Mix dry ingredients in medium bowl.
2. Stir in carrots and onion.
3. In blender, blend tofu and liquid amino acids until smooth and creamy.
4. Add wet ingredients to the bowl. Mix well. Then form into patties.
5. Brown slowly in a non-stick pan. If baking, bake at 400° F for 8-10 minutes on each side or until golden brown.

GRILLED BEAN BURGERS

Preparation Time: 15-20 minutes   *Difficulty: Easy*   *Serves: 8 patties*

INGREDIENTS:
- 1 large onion, chopped
- 4 minced garlic cloves
- 2 medium carrots, shredded
- 1 ½ tsp. chili powder
- 1 tsp. cumin
- 2 cups black beans (15 oz. can rinsed)
- 1 ½ cups quick oats
- 2 tbsp. Dijon or spicy brown mustard
- 2 tbsp. reduced sodium soy sauce
- 2 tbsp. ketchup
- ¼ tsp. pepper (optional)

DIRECTIONS:

1. In a sprayed, non-stick pan, sauté onion and garlic on low heat about 2 minutes.
2. Add carrot, chili powder, and cumin, Cook for 2 more minutes. Remove from heat.
3. In a separate bowl, partially mash beans. Stir in oats, mustard, and ketchup.
4. Add warm ingredients from pan to bowl. Mix.
5. Form into 8 patties.
6. Spray grill with cooking spray. Grill covered for 4-5 minutes on each side or until heated through.

HINT: Serve with buns, lettuce, and salsa, or with your favorite burger toppings.

HAYSTACKS

Preparation Time: 5 minutes + sauce recipe time   *Difficulty: Easy*   *Serves: 2-4*

INGREDIENTS:
- Baked corn chips
- Brown rice
- 1 cup cooked pinto beans
- 1 recipe of **Cashew Pimento Cheese Spread** or **Delightful Tofu Dill Dip**
- Shredded lettuce
- Chopped tomatoes
- Chopped onions
- Sprouts
- Olives

DIRECTIONS:

1. Layer ingredients in bowls in order listed. Use what proportions of ingredients you like.

LIMA BEANS WITH DILL AND ONION

Preparation Time: 30 minutes + 60-minute cook time   *Difficulty: Easy*   *Serves: 6-8*

INGREDIENTS:
- 2 lbs. fresh, frozen lima beans
- 2 cups onion, chopped
- 2 tbsp. dill weed or fresh dill
- 1/3 cup olive oil
- 3-4 tbsp. water
- 1 ½ tsp. salt

DIRECTIONS:

1. Cover lima beans in water and boil in medium-large pot for 15 minutes.
2. In non-stick pan, sauté onions in oil and water.
3. Drain almost all of the water from lima beans.
4. Add the onions to the pot, along with the dill.
5. Simmer on low for 10 minutes.
6. Add salt when tender, if desired.
7. Serve over brown rice, couscous, or zwieback.

HINTS: This can also be done in the oven. Put beans in a casserole dish, covering with about 1" of water. Add the onions and dill. Bake at 350° F for about an hour, or until tender. Stir in oil and salt when tender.

MILLET TOMATO LOAF

Preparation Time: 5-10 minutes + 90-minute cook time   *Difficulty: Easy*   *Serves: 4-6*

INGREDIENTS:
- 4 cups tomato juice
- 1 cup onion, chopped into chunks
- ½ cup raw cashews
- 1 can black olives, chopped
- 1 cup millet (uncooked)
- ½ tsp. marjoram
- ½ tsp. sage
- ½ tsp. salt

DIRECTIONS:

1. Blend smooth 1 cup of the juice with the onion and cashews.
2. Stir together with all remaining ingredients.
3. Pour into a sprayed 9" x 13" baking dish.
4. Cover with foil and bake at 350° F for 75 minutes.
5. Remove foil, and continue to bake for 10 more minutes.

PIZZA

Preparation Time: 20-30 minutes   *Difficulty: Easy*   *Serves: varies*

CRUST OPTIONS:
- English muffins
- Store-bought crust, such as Mama Mia's
- Pita Bread
- Homemade dough

TOPPING OPTIONS:
- Low-fat, low-sugar, low-sodium tomato sauce
- Mock Mozzarella, Velvet Cheese, Soy Cheese, or our **Agar Cheese** recipe
- Sautéed or fresh mushrooms, onions, black olives, peppers, garlic, fresh basil, etc.
- Morning Star sausage crumbles, vegetarian bacon bits, or our **Burger Delight** recipe
- Tofu, crumbled and seasoned to taste

DIRECTIONS:

1. Layer sauce and toppings as desired on bread of your choice.
2. Bake at 350° F for 15-20 minutes, watching for burning.

SLOPPY JOES

Preparation Time: 15-20 minutes   *Difficulty: Easy*   *Serves: 4*

INGREDIENTS:

- 1 chopped onion
- 16 oz. frozen vegetarian meat crumbles or our **Burger Delight** recipe
- ½ cup water
- 6 oz. tomato paste
- 3 tsp. tamari
- 1 tbsp. vegetarian Worcestershire sauce
- 2 tsp. brown sugar
- 4 whole grain buns
- 1 sliced onion (optional)
- sliced dill pickles (optional)

DIRECTIONS:

1. Sauté onion on high heat in a non-stick skillet for 3 minutes, or until translucent.
2. Add the veggie meat crumbles and ¼ cup of water to the skillet and cook for 5 more minutes.
3. Stir in the tomato paste. Add the remaining water and stir until thoroughly mixed, using more water as necessary to make a thick sauce.
4. Stir in the tamari, Worcestershire, and sugar.
5. Place a generous amount of filling into each bun. Top with sliced onions and pickles.

HINT: Steamed spinach and potato wedges make great sides for these Sloppy Joes.

THAI CURRY

Preparation Time: 25-30 minutes   *Difficulty: Moderate*   *Serves: 3-5*

CURRY INGREDIENTS:
- 1 tbsp. coconut oil
- 1 sliced small onion
- ½ tbsp. fresh ground ginger or ginger powder
- 1-2 cloves of minced garlic
- 14-15 oz. can of light coconut milk (or 2 cups)
- ½ cup water
- 2-3 tbsp. vegan curry paste (red, green, or yellow)
- 1 tbsp. soy sauce
- ¼ cup tomato sauce
- 1 tbsp. coconut or brown sugar
- 1-2 kaffir lime leaves or ½ small bay leaf and ½ tbsp. lime juice and a hint of lime zest (peel)
- 1 leaf of lemongrass (optional)
- ½ tsp. ground turmeric
- 2 cups diced red potatoes
- 2-3 carrots sliced at about ¼" thickness and then cut into 2"– 3" lengths
- 1 ½ cups asparagus with ends removed and cut into 2"– 3" lengths
- 1 cup of chopped peppers (red, yellow, and/or orange)
- ½ cup sliced or whole mushrooms (optional)
- ½ cup tofu cut into cubes (optional)

SERVE WITH:

- cooked wild rice or multigrain rice
- garnish with Thai basil and/or cilantro, chopped onions, and chopped cashews or peanuts

DIRECTIONS:

1. Melt the coconut oil in the pan over medium heat.
2. Sauté the onion slices until translucent.
3. Add the garlic and ginger. Stir and cook until fragrant.
4. Stir in the coconut milk, water, curry paste, soy sauce, sugar, turmeric, tomato sauce, carrot, and potatoes. At this point, you can also add the lemongrass, lime leaves (or bay leaf with lime zest).
5. Reach a boil, then reduce heat and simmer until potatoes are nearly tender. Stir occasionally.
6. Add the asparagus and peppers, and, optionally, the tofu and/or mushrooms, and cook until all vegetables are tender. Keep stirring occasionally.
7. Taste and season more as needed.
8. Serve over rice with garnishes. Usually, you don't eat the lemongrass or the leaves.

HINT: Water chestnuts, baby corns, or other vegetables can be added. Asian vegetable blends can also be used, but might be mushy if frozen.

TOFU RICE

Preparation Time: 20-30 minutes   *Difficulty: Easy*   *Serves: 4*

INGREDIENTS:

- 1 pkg. firm tofu
- 4 tbsp. Bragg's Liquid Amino Acids or soy sauce
- 4 cloves chopped garlic
- 3 cups cooked brown rice
- 1 tbsp. olive oil
- 1 thinly-sliced onion

DIRECTIONS:

1. Mix Bragg's and garlic in a large zipper bag and shake well.
2. Cube tofu into small pieces, about ½" cubes.
3. Add the tofu to the bag, mix well without crumbling the tofu too much, and marinate over night.
4. Sauté marinated tofu in olive oil, saving extra tofu marinade for later.
5. Add onion and cook until clear.
6. Add extra marinade and hot, cooked rice.
7. Stir together and season to your taste.

HINT: Other vegetables can be added to this, like sliced mushrooms, green peppers, and shaved carrots.

VEGAN ENCHILADAS

Preparation Time: 20-30 minutes   *Difficulty: Easy*   *Serves: 4-6*

INGREDIENTS:
- 1 chopped onion
- 1 chopped zucchini
- 2 shredded carrots
- 1 cup vegan cheddar cheese, shredded
- 1 package vegan soy grounds or soy curls
- 12 corn tortillas
- 16 oz. salsa or enchilada sauce
- 1 ½ cups black beans
- cilantro to taste

DIRECTIONS:

1. Cover the bottom of a baking dish with onions and zucchini. Coat with some salsa or enchilada sauce.
2. Cover with 4 corn tortillas.
3. Cover the tortillas with sauce, soy grounds, and 1/3 of the cheese.
4. Place another layer of tortillas with sauce, beans, carrots, and 1/3 of the cheese.
5. Put a final layer of tortilla, covering with sauce and cheese.
6. Bake at 350° F for 25 minutes, or until cheese has all melted.
7. Sprinkle fresh cilantro on top and serve.

HINT: You can also add baby spinach in with the soy grounds for added flavor.

VEGAN SPRING ROLLS

Preparation Time: 20-30 minutes   Difficulty: Moderate   Serves: 3-4+

SPRING ROLL INGREDIENTS:

- 1 package rice paper spring roll wrappers (Asian supermarkets carry them. They look like translucent disks about the size of a saucer)
- 1 small bag spring lettuces
- 1 cup baby sweet peppers chopped into slices
- 1 cucumber, sliced into strips 3-4" long
- 1 avocado, peeled and sliced
- ½ cup shredded carrots
- ½ cup thin-sliced purple cabbage
- 1 sliced tomato
- Fresh lime to squeeze (optional)
- Thai basil or cilantro to taste (optional)
- Cooked beans or tofu (optional)

DIPPING SAUCE INGREDIENTS:

- ¼ cup your favorite nut butter
- 1 tbsp. soy sauce
- ¼ tbsp. minced ginger
- ½ clove minced garlic
- 1 tbsp. rice vinegar
- ¼ tsp. Sriracha or Asian hot sauce
- ¼ tsp. maple syrup
- 1/6 cup water (1/2 of your 1/3 measuring cup)

DIRECTIONS:

1. Slice and prepare veggies for the rolls.
2. Open the pack of spring roll wrappers.
3. On a large plate or flat-bottomed skillet, pour warm water (not hot) about ½" deep.
4. Place a rice paper wrap in the water until softened, about 5-10 seconds.
5. Lay out the wrapper on a clean surface or cutting board.
6. Layer the ingredients you want inside the wrap, making a mound toward the middle.
7. Fold the rice paper snugly over the ingredients. Fold both ends down over it, and roll like a burrito.
8. Whisk together all sauce ingredients until smooth. It thickens with time. Check flavoring and adjust to make it thinner, nuttier, spicier, etc.
9. Dip the wraps in the sauce and enjoy!

HINT: Experiment with seasonings, like cumin, cayenne pepper, or hints of curry for variety.

VEGGIE STIR FRY

Preparation Time: 15-25 minutes   *Difficulty: Easy*   *Serves: 4*

INGREDIENTS:

- ½ cup pineapple juice
- 1 tbsp. sugar
- 1 tbsp. lemon juice
- 1 tbsp. corn starch
- 1 tsp. soy sauce
- ½ tbsp. olive oil
- ½ cup chopped scallions
- 1 cup broccoli florets
- 1 cup cauliflower florets
- 1 cup sliced carrots
- 1 cup sliced celery
- 1 cup half-moon sliced zucchini
- 1 cup sliced red peppers
- 1 tsp. chopped garlic

DIRECTIONS:

1. Combine the first 5 ingredients in a bowl. Mix and set aside.
2. In a large pan or wok over medium heat, add scallions, broccoli, cauliflower, carrots, garlic, and celery. Stir and cook for about 2 minutes.
3. Add zucchini and peppers to mixture and stir.
4. Cover pan for 1 minute.
5. Add sauce and stir.
6. Bring to a boil for 1 minute and cook 1 minute, keep covered.
7. Serve immediately.

ZUCCHINI BURGERS

Preparation Time: 45-60 minutes   *Difficulty: Moderate*   *Serves: 6-10 patties*

INGREDIENTS:

- 2 cups grated zucchini
- 1 ½ tbsp. Bill's Best Seasoning
- ½ tsp. salt
- 1 small onion, minced
- 1 clove garlic, minced
- 1 finely-grated carrot
- 1/3 cup walnuts, chopped fine
- ¼ cup nutritional yeast flakes
- 1 cup quick oats
- ½ cup gluten flour or 1 tbsp. ground chia seeds mixed with 3 tbsp. water

DIRECTIONS:

1. Place zucchini in a medium-sized bowl. Mix with Bill's Best Seasoning and salt. Set aside.
2. Chop the other veggies.
3. In another bowl, mix together the walnuts, yeast flakes, oats, and the flour (or chia seed mixture).
4. Add the chopped veggies and seasoned zucchini to the second bowl, mixing well.
5. Use a large-mouth jar ring to make burger-sized patties, packing the mixture into the ring to make the shape. Make the patties on a sprayed baking sheet.
6. Bake at 350° F for 15 minutes, flip them carefully, and then bake for another 15-20 minutes on the other side until lightly browned.

HINT: These also freeze well.

SOUPS, SALADS, & SIDES

RECIPES FOR HEALTHY LIVING

15 BEAN SOUP

Preparation Time: 10-15 minutes + cook time   *Difficulty: Easy*   *Serves: 4-6*

INGREDIENTS:
- 1 pkg. Hurst 15 Bean Soup (or comparable bean soup mix)
- 3 quarts water or 2 quarts if you pre-soak beans
- 1 cup chopped carrots
- 1 cup chopped celery
- 1 medium onion, chopped
- 4-8 cloves minced garlic
- 1-2 tbsp. McKay's Vegetarian Chicken Seasoning, Bill's Best Chik'nish, or Veggie Better Than Bullion
- ¼ cup McCormick's Imitation Bac'n Pieces
- 1 tbsp. liquid smoke
- 1 tsp. basil (optional)
- 1 tsp. tarragon (optional)
- 1 finely-chopped serrano pepper (optional)

DIRECTIONS:
1. Throw away the seasoning packet that comes with the beans.
2. Place beans and seasonings in a crock pot and cover until water is 1-2" deep.
3. Cook overnight on high.
4. Add veggies in the morning and cook on low for about 4 hours.

BAKED POTATOES

Preparation Time: 5 minutes + potato cook time   *Difficulty: Easy*   *Serves: 1 per potato*

DIRECTIONS:
1. Top your baked potatoes with leftovers from one of these recipes from this cookbook:

TOPPING RECIPES:
- Alfredo Sauce
- Avocado Mayo
- Cashew Pimento Cheese Dip
- Country Style Gravy
- Delightful Tofu Dill Spread
- Hummus
- Kale Soup
- Lentil Soup

COLESLAW

Preparation Time: 15-20 minutes   *Difficulty: Easy*   *Serves: 5-8 or as a side*

INGREDIENTS:

- 4 cups shredded green cabbage
- 4 cups shredded red cabbage
- 2 cups grated carrots
- 2 tbsp. sesame seeds
- 1 tbsp. dill flakes
- ½ cup tofu mayonnaise
- ¼ cup soy milk
- 2 tbsp. vinegar or lemon juice
- 1 tsp. cane sugar

DIRECTIONS:

1. Place cabbage, carrots, sesames seeds, and dill in a salad bowl. Toss well.
2. Mix mayo with soy milk. Pour over slaw. Mix well.
3. Add the sugar with the vinegar or lemon juice. Mix well. Serve.

CRUNCHY SOY-CORN SALAD

Preparation Time: 10-15 minutes   *Difficulty: Easy*   *Serves: 3-4 or as a side*

SALAD INGREDIENTS:

- 12 oz. pkg. shelled green soybeans (edamame)
- 16 oz. frozen sweet corn
- 1 cup cubed jicama or water chestnuts
- 2/3 cup diced celery
- ½ cup diced sweet red pepper
- 1/3 cup green onion, sliced to about ¼"
- 1 tbsp. minced fresh parsley or cilantro

DRESSING INGREDIENTS:

- 5 tbsp. fresh lemon juice
- 1 tbsp. honey
- 1 ½ tsp. salt
- ¼ tsp. garlic powder
- ¼ tsp. dry basil
- 1/8 tsp. dill weed

DIRECTIONS:

1. Mix corn soybeans, jicama, celery, red pepper, onion, and parsley.
2. Combine dressing ingredients, mixing well.
3. Mix dressing with veggies. Chill and serve.

*Recipe adapted from *Vital Vittles* by Heather Leno (www.HeatherLeno.com)

DILLY CARROTS AND GREEN BEANS

Preparation Time: 20-30 minutes　　*Difficulty: Easy*　　*Serves: 1-2 or as a side*

INGREDIENTS:

- ½ lb. fresh green beans or frozen string beans (cut and trimmed)
- ½ - ¾ cups boiling water
- 1 tsp. sugar or stevia
- ½ tsp salt
- ½ tsp. dill weed
- 4 medium carrots cut into thin strips 2-3" long

DIRECTIONS:

1. Add green beans, sugar, salt, and dill to boiling water.
2. Simmer 5 minutes. Then add the carrots.
3. Simmer until both are tender, about 10 minutes. Serve hot.

EASY BEAN SALAD

Preparation Time: 10-15 minutes　　*Difficulty: Easy*　　*Serves: 3-5 or as a side*

INGREDIENTS:

- 1 ½ cups cooked or canned kidney beans, rinsed and drained
- 1 ½ cups cooked or canned pinto beans, rinsed and drained
- 1 ½ cups cooked or canned black-eyed peas, rinsed and drained
- 10 oz. pkg. frozen lima beans, thawed or edamame
- 1 cup frozen corn, thawed or cooked, fresh corn
- 1 diced large red pepper
- ½ diced medium red onion
- ½ cup low-fat or fat-free Italian salad dressing or our **Good Seasons Italian Dressing** Recipe
- 1 tsp. salt
- 1 tsp. ground black pepper

DIRECTIONS:

1. Combine all ingredients in a large bowl and toss gently.
2. Serve cold or at room temperature.

HINT: Can be stored for up to 3 days if a container in the fridge.

* Adapted from *The Get Healthy, Go Vegan Cookbook* by Neal Barnard, M.D. and Robyn Webb

GREAT GREENS

Preparation Time: 30-40 minutes　　　*Difficulty: Easy*　　　*Serves: 3-4 or as a side*

INGREDIENTS:
- Large bag of fresh greens
- Water
- 3 tbsp. vegetarian chicken seasoning
- 2 tbsp. garlic powder
- 2 tbsp. onion powder
- 2 tbsp. sweet basil
- Bragg's Liquid Amino Acids or Soy Sauce
- Olive oil
- 2 coarsely-chopped onions
- 5 cloves minced garlic

DIRECTIONS:
1. Rinse greens. Then cut greens into bite-sized pieces and place in a large pot.
2. Cover with water and add spices to the pot.
3. Simmer until tender, approximately 20-30 minutes.
4. Drain in a colander, saving broth for a soup base, if desired.
5. Sauté onion and garlic in olive oil.
6. Stir drained greens into onion and garlic mixture.
7. Season to taste with Bragg's or soy sauce. Serve.

KALE SOUP

Preparation Time: 40-50 minutes   *Difficulty: Moderate*   *Serves: 3-4 or as a side*

INGREDIENTS:

- 1 bunch kale (savoy cabbage works as a substitute)
- 1 ¼ cup water for boiling kale
- 3 finely-chopped medium onions
- 6 large stalks of celery with leaves, finely-chopped
- 3 tbsp. olive oil
- 1 lb. peeled and sliced carrots
- 5 large Idaho potatoes or Florida red potatoes, washed and diced (do not peel)
- 4-6 more cups of water for stock
- Veggie Chicken Seasoning to taste
- 2 cans cannelloni beans, red kidney beans, or white beans

DIRECTIONS:

1. Wash kale and remove stems. Cut into bite-sized pieces.
2. Cook kale in 1 ¼ cup water until tender.
3. Sauté celery and onions in oil.
4. Add carrots and potatoes to celery and onions.
5. Cover and cook until potatoes begin to show translucent spots. Flip them several times as you cook.
6. Add 4-6 cups water to the vegetables, depending on how thick you want the soup to be. You can always add more later.
7. Add vegetarian chicken seasoning to taste. Add it a little at a time.
8. Bring to boil, then simmer until potatoes are tender.
9. Drain kale and add it to soup with the 2 cans of drained beans.
10. Simmer 20-30 minutes. Serve hot.

LENTIL SOUP

Preparation Time: 40-50 minutes   *Difficulty: Moderate*   *Serves: 6-8 or as a side*

INGREDIENTS:
- 3 cups small brown lentils
- 6 cups of water
- 8 more cups of water
- 3 bay leaves
- 1 tsp. oregano
- 1 chopped large onion
- 4-6 cloves chopped garlic
- 1 ½ cups chopped red, yellow, and green bell peppers
- 15 oz. can tomato sauce
- salt to taste
- ¼ cup olive oil (optional)

DIRECTIONS:

1. Bring the 3 cups of lentils in a large Dutch oven with the 6 cups of water to a boil.
2. Add cold tap water to the pot. The lentils should sink. Carefully pour off all water.
3. Add 8 cups of new water, the bay leaves, oregano, onion, and garlic. Then simmer until lentils are tender, about 20 minutes.
4. Add the can of tomato sauce. Cook for 5 more minutes. Add water if soup is too thick.
5. Add salt to taste, and the olive oil, if desired.

QUINOA SALAD

Preparation Time: 45-50 minutes   Difficulty: Easy   Serves: 6-8 or as a side

SALAD INGREDIENTS:
- 1 ½ cups quinoa
- 2 ½ cups water
- ½ cup sliced green onions
- 2 oz. sliced, black olives
- 1 ½ cups diced tomato
- 1 ½ cups diced English cucumber
- 1 ½ cups chopped red, green, and yellow bell peppers

DRESSING INGREDIENTS:
- ¼ cup olive oil
- 1/3 cup lemon juice
- 1 tsp. garlic powder
- 1 tsp. Italian herbs
- ¼ cup dried onion flakes
- ½ tsp. oregano
- ½ tsp. basil

DIRECTIONS:

1. Wash quinoa very well under faucet in a fine mesh colander.
2. In a medium pot, bring water to boil. Add quinoa.
3. Cover and simmer approximately 15 minutes, or until water is all absorbed.
4. Remove from heat and add remaining ingredients to cooled quinoa. Chill.
5. Mix together dressing ingredients thoroughly.
6. Toss over salad and allow it to marinade 30 minutes in refrigerator before serving.

HINT: Great in a pita pocket with hummus!

ROASTED VEGGIES

Preparation Time: 30-45 minutes   Difficulty: Easy   Serves: 3-4 or as a side

INGREDIENTS:

- 2 red peppers cut into strips
- 1 green pepper cut into strips
- 1 yellow squash sliced diagonally
- 1 zucchini sliced diagonally
- 1 onion (sweet or red), quartered
- 1 can or jar of artichoke hearts (not the ones packed in brine), drained

SEASONING INGREDIENTS:

- 1 tsp. thyme
- ½ tsp. salt
- garlic salt or celery salt to taste

DIRECTIONS:

1. Preheat oven to 450° F.
2. Coat cookie sheet or roaster pan with spray or olive oil.
3. Toss veggies in a plastic bag with just enough olive oil to coat them lightly.
4. Arrange veggies in an even layer on the pan.
5. Sprinkle with seasoning.
6. Bake for 20-30 minutes at 450° F. Shake the pan or carefully flip veggies 1-2 times to prevent scorching.

HINTS: Great served over whole grains or in a sandwich wrap. Eat with beans or tofu for protein. Great as leftovers, too.

ROASTED GARLIC

Preparation Time: 2-5 minutes + cook time   Difficulty: Easy   Serves: 1, or as a garnish

INGREDIENTS:

- 1 or more whole bulbs of garlic, unpeeled

DIRECTIONS:

1. Put whole bulb of garlic in a sprayed baking dish.
2. Bake for 45-60 minutes at 350° F.
3. Remove from oven and pop garlic cloves out of skin. Eat as a spread.

SCALLOPED POTATOES

Preparation Time: 15-20 minutes + cook time   *Difficulty: Easy*   *Serves: 6-8*

INGREDIENTS:

- 1 cup raw, washed cashews
- 3 cups water
- 2 tsp. salt
- 1 tsp. basil
- 2 tsp. onion powder
- 1 tsp. garlic powder
- 4-6 cups sliced, raw potatoes
- 2 cups sliced onion
- 2 tbsp. nutritional yeast flakes

DIRECTIONS:

1. Blend 1 cup of water with 1 cup cashews until very creamy.
2. Add remainder of spices and water, and blend again.
3. Layer sliced potatoes and onions in a sprayed 9" x 13" baking dish.
4. Pour cashew mixture over potatoes and onions.
5. Cover and bake at 350° F for 1 hr.
6. Uncover and continue to bake until liquid is absorbed and potatoes are tender, approximately 30 more minutes.

DESSERTS & SWEETS

RECIPES FOR HEALTHY LIVING

APPLE ICING BREAD

Preparation Time: 15-20 minutes + rising time & bake time   *Difficulty: Moderate*   *Serves: 3-5*

INGREDIENTS:

- One recipe of whole wheat bread dough
- 3-4 cups unsweetened applesauce
- ¾ cup raisins
- ½ cup unsweetened coconut
- Cinnamon or pie spice to taste (optional)

DIRECTIONS:

1. Spread bread dough on sprayed pizza pan or cookie sheet.
2. Sprinkle with raisins.
3. Spread applesauce on top.
4. Sprinkle coconut on top.
5. Optionally, sprinkle cinnamon or pie spices to taste on top.
6. Let the dough rise in a warm spot for an hour.
7. Preheat oven and bake in at 350° F for 25 minutes.

HINT: You can also drizzle our **Cashew Maple Crème** recipe on top of it.

AMBROSIA SALAD

Preparation Time: 15-20 minutes   *Difficulty: Easy*   *Serves: 3-4*

INGREDIENTS:
- 2 oranges, peeled and chopped
- 2 cups pineapple chunks, drained (save some juice for later)
- 1 sliced banana
- ¼ cup unsweetened, shredded coconut
- 2 – 4 tbsp. dried cranberries
- 1 – 3 tbsp. leftover juice from chopping fruit (use less if salad is too wet)
- 1 tbsp. water
- ½ tsp. almond extract

DIRECTIONS:

1. Combine the oranges, pineapple, banana, coconut, and cranberries in a medium bowl.
2. Mix water, almond extract, and leftover juice from chopped fruit in a separate bowl.
3. Pour the liquid over the fruit and toss carefully.
4. Refrigerate in a covered container. Eat within a day, or within 2 days without bananas.

HINT: Try mixing in other chopped fruit, like kiwis, cherries, or blackberries.

* Adapted from *The Get Healthy, Go Vegan Cookbook* by Neal Barnard, M.D. and Robyn Webb

BLUEBERRY PIE

Preparation Time: 30-40 minutes + cooling time   *Difficulty: Moderate*   *Serves: 8*

CRUST INGREDIENTS:

- 1 cup chopped dates
- 1/3 cup water
- ¾ cup Grape Nuts Cereal
- ½ cup quick oats
- ¼ cup finely-ground pecans

FILLING INGREDIENTS:

- 2 cups frozen blueberries
- 1 cup frozen grape juice concentrate
- ¼ cup minute tapioca
- 1 tsp. vanilla extract
- 1 tbsp. lemon juice

DIRECTIONS:

1. Place dates and water in a small pot. Bring to a boil.
2. Simmer dates until they are soft. Mash them.
3. Place dates in a mixing bowl. Add remaining crust ingredients and mix well with fork.
4. Press into the bottom of a pie plate and up the sides.
5. Bake at 350° F for 12 minutes. Cool to room temperature.
6. For the filling, place the grape juice and tapioca in a medium pot. Let stand for 5 minutes.
7. Bring the pot to a boil, and then reduce the heat and simmer for 5 minutes.
8. Add blueberries, lemon juice, and vanilla to the pot.
9. Simmer for 5 more minutes, or until the tapioca becomes clear.
10. Pour mixture into crust in pie plate. Chill in refrigerator until firm.

CAROB CHIP CANDY

Preparation Time: 50-60 minutes   *Difficulty: Easy*   *Serves: varies*

INGREDIENTS:
- 1 cup organic peanut or almond butter
- 3 cups non-dairy, barley malt sweetened carob chips
- 1 cup unsweetened coconut or 3 cups Rice Krispies cereal (optional)

DIRECTIONS:
1. Spread nut butter in crock pot.
2. Sprinkle carob chips on top and heat on low for about 45 minutes.
3. Stir when carob is shiny and beginning to melt.
4. Continue to stir until the chips become smooth and spread throughout mixture.
5. Optionally, add Rice Krispies or coconut at this point.
6. Drop mixture by spoonful on waxed paper covered cookie sheet or into candy molds.

CAROB PIE

Preparation Time: 30-45 minutes   *Difficulty: Easy*   *Serves: 6-8*

INGREDIENTS:
- 4 cups cashew milk
- ½ cup honey or agave or 1 cup date butter
- 6 tbsp. corn starch
- 1 tsp. Roma coffee substitute
- 6 tbsp. carob powder
- ½ tsp salt
- 1 tbsp. vanilla
- ¼ cup unsweetened coconut
- baked pie shell

DIRECTIONS:
1. Make cashew milk by blending 1 cup cashews with 1 cup water until creamy. Then add water to make 4 cups total.
2. Add remaining ingredients (except coconut) and blend on high until creamy.
3. Pour into a saucepan and cook over medium heat, stirring constantly with a wire whisk until thick.
4. Remove from heat and pour into a baked pie shell, such as our **Granola Crumb Crust** recipe.
5. Sprinkle with coconut and chill overnight before serving.

CASHEW MAPLE CRÈME

Preparation Time: 30-45 minutes   Difficulty: Easy   Serves: 6-8

INGREDIENTS:

- 1 ½ cup whole raw cashews
- ½ cup maple syrup or agave nectar
- ¼ cup fresh lemon juice
- 2 tbsp. cold-pressed coconut oil or coconut butter (optional)
- ½ tsp. fresh, scraped vanilla bean or 1 tsp. pure alcohol-free vanilla extract
- ¼ tsp. sea salt (Celtic Sea Salt if available)
- 2 tbsp. fresh lemon and lime zest

DIRECTIONS:

1. Soak cashews in filtered water 4-6 hours, and then strain.
2. Blend the strained cashews, maple syrup, fresh lemon juice, coconut oil, vanilla, and sea salt at high speed in your blender. If your blender can't get stuff moving well, add a small amount of water so you can blend until at an even consistency.
3. Once smooth, fold in the fresh lemon and lime zest.
4. Chill, and depending on the thickness, use as a spread or a drizzle for cake and bread.

FIVE-MINUTE CAROB CAKE

Preparation Time: 5 minutes + bake time   *Difficulty: Easy*   *Serves: 3-5*

INGREDIENTS:

- 1 cup Florida Crystals raw sugar
- 1 ½ cup unsifted, unbleached white flour
- ½ tsp. salt
- ¼ cup carob powder
- 1 tsp. baking soda
- 1 tbsp. lemon juice
- 1/3 cup oil or coconut oil
- 1 tsp almond flavoring
- 1 cup water with 1 tsp. Roma coffee, steeped and cooled

DIRECTIONS:

1. Mix ingredients in order given. Stir until at an even consistency.
2. Pour mixture into ungreased 8" square cake pan.
3. Bake at 350° F for 30-35 minutes.
4. Frost, serve plain with berries, or drizzle with our **Cashew Maple Crème** recipe.

FRUIT SMOOTHIES

Preparation Time: 5-10 minutes   *Difficulty: Easy*   *Serves: 1-2*

INGREDIENTS:

- 1 cup vanilla soy milk
- 1 cup frozen fruit
- 1 tbsp. ground flax seed
- 1 frozen banana, broken or chopped into pieces
- 2 tsp. sweetener of your choice, such as agave or a pinch of stevia

DIRECTIONS:

1. Put all ingredients in the blender.
2. Blend until smooth.
3. Add more milk if too thick.
4. Enjoy immediately.

HINTS: Try a variety of frozen fruits. Bananas help thicken the recipe. Fresh fruit can also be used, but frozen ones make it frostier. You can also try other non-dairy milks.

GRANOLA CRUMB CRUST

Preparation Time: 30-40 minutes   *Difficulty: Easy*   *Serves: 6-8 with filling*

INGREDIENTS:

- 4 cups granola (ground down to 3 cups)
- 2 tsp. coriander
- 1 tsp. cinnamon
- 3-4 tbsp. applesauce
- 2 tbsp. water
- pinch of salt

DIRECTIONS:

1. Blend 2 cups of granola on high until fine. It should yield about 1 ½ cups of ground granola.
2. Pour into bowl and repeat until you have 3 cups of ground granola.
3. Add remaining ingredients.
4. Stir together with fork and then mix together with your hands.
5. Press into bottom and sides of 9" x 13" baking dish.
6. Bake at 350° F for 25 minutes.

LEMON PIE

Preparation Time: 15-20 minutes   *Difficulty: Easy*   *Serves: 6-8*

INGREDIENTS:

- 3 cups unsweetened pineapple juice
- ½ cup orange juice concentrate
- 6 tbsp. corn starch
- 7 tbsp. honey or agave
- 1/8 tsp. salt
- 6 tbsp. lemon juice
- 1 tsp. imitation butter flavor (optional)
- 1 tsp. lemon extract (optional)
- ¼ cup unsweetened coconut

DIRECTIONS:

1. Blend all ingredients for 20 seconds.
2. Empty into sauce pan and cook over medium-high heat, stirring constantly until thick.
3. Pour into baked pie shell, such as our **Granola Crumb Crust** recipe.
4. Sprinkle with coconut. Chill and serve.

*Adapted from *Country Life Cookbook*, page 55.*

OUTRAGEOUS CORN MUFFINS

Preparation Time: 30-40 minutes   *Difficulty: Easy*   *Serves: 12 muffins*

DRY INGREDIENTS:

- 1/3 cup corn meal
- 1/3 cup soy, spelt, or oat flour
- 1 cup whole wheat pastry flour
- ¼ cup wheat germ
- 1 tsp. baking soda
- ½ tsp. salt
- 1 cup ground almonds.

WET INGREDIENTS:

- 1 tbsp. egg substitute
- ¾ cup soy milk
- 1 tbsp. lemon juice
- ½ cup applesauce
- 6 tbsp. orange juice concentrate
- ½ cup raisins or currants.
- ½ cup diced dried apricots
- 1/3 cup honey
- 2 tsp. vanilla

DIRECTIONS:

1. Mix dry ingredients together in a large bowl.
2. Combine liquid ingredients in a separate bowl. Mix.
3. Stir into dry ingredients until the batter is moist and lumpy. Do not over stir.
4. Scoop into oiled or paper-lined muffin tins until 2/3 full.
5. Bake at 350° F for 25 minutes.

*Adapted from a recipe by *Bob's Red Mill*.

STUFFED MEDJOOL DATES

Preparation Time: 10-15 minutes   *Difficulty: Easy*   *Serves: varies*

INGREDIENTS:

- Large Medjool Dates
- Pecans, almonds, walnuts, or other nuts
- Nut butter of your choice

DIRECTIONS:

1. Remove pits from dates.
2. Fill opening with a dab of nut butter of your choice and your favorite raw nuts.
3. Arrange on a platter and enjoy!

HINTS: Stuff with pineapple. You can also roll the stuffed dates in very fine coconut.

SWEET POTATO SALAD

Preparation Time: 10-15 minutes   *Difficulty: Easy*   *Serves: varies*

INGREDIENTS:

- 3 cups clean sweet potatoes
- 1 can crushed pineapple in juice
- 1 tsp. cinnamon
- ¼ tsp. ground cloves
- ¼ tsp. allspice
- ½ cup chopped nuts
- ½ cup raisins

DIRECTIONS:

1. Skin and shred raw sweet potatoes.
2. Add other ingredients and toss until mixed.
3. Let marinate 2-3 hours before serving. Salad can be chilled.

RESOURCES

RECIPES FOR HEALTHY LIVING

THINGS TO ALWAYS HAVE IN YOUR PANTRY

PLANNING AHEAD IS THE KEY TO SUCCESS!

INGREDIENTS TO ALWAYS HAVE ON HAND:

- Whole grains
- Whole grain breads
- Fresh fruits & vegetables
- Sweet potatoes
- White potatoes
- Canned beans
- Nut butters
- Applesauce
- Raisins
- Herbal teas
- Braggs Liquid Amino Acids
- Yeast flakes
- Tofu
- Homemade vegan cheeses
- Hot whole grain cereals
- Hummus
- Salad dressing
- Frozen patties
- Waffles
- Cut-up veggies
- Cold teas
- Brown rice
- Oatmeal
- Nuts
- Your favorite seasonings

BEST STORE-BOUGHT CEREAL OPTIONS

PLANNING AHEAD IS THE KEY TO SUCCESS!

HEALTHIEST CHOICES FOR COLD CEREALS:
- Flax Plus Cereals – all varieties
- Shredded Wheat
- All Bran
- Bran Flakes (any brand – read labels first)
- Grape Nuts
- Grape Nut Flakes
- Plain Cheerios
- Kashi "Go Lean" – all varieties

HINT: Avoid all store-bought granolas as a breakfast, as they are closer to dessert than cereal.

BEST HEALTHY SNACKING OPTIONS

EATING CAREFULLY WHEN YOU NEED A LITTLE SOMETHING EXTRA

SNACK	BENEFITS
EDAMAME	A good energy snack with healthy fats, protein, and lots of vitamins.
PUMPKIN SEEDS	Sugar-free treat with good protein.
CELERY	Mostly water with some vitamins, it's low calorie. Also great with nut butters.
PISTACHIOS	Eat them in the shell, so you eat less. Good source of fiber and B vitamins.
FROZEN GRAPES	Sweet treats like these can satisfy that sweet tooth! Good for antioxidants.
APRICOTS	Low in sugar, but with good fiber.
KALE CHIPS	Nutrient rich, Kale chips can satisfy that urge to munch and crunch.
FRESH BERRIES	A handful of fresh berries is high in antioxidants, and pleasantly tart or sweet.
HUMMUS	Dip chopped veggies or mini tomatoes for a filling, healthy snack.
SWEET PEPPERS	Very high in vitamins A and C, they're also a good source of many other vitamins and minerals.
TRAIL MIX	Nuts and dried fruit offer a good balance of fat, protein, and carbohydrates.
SLICED VEGGIES	High-moisture veggies like cucumbers can be filling. Add a few mini tomatoes, some celery, or carrots for variety and texture.
DRIED PRUNES	Make sure to get no sugar added dried prunes. Eat just a couple. They're sweet, but a great source of fiber.
AVOCADO	Eat half an avocado with a few slices or sticks of your favorite colorful vegetables to get your healthy fats, fiber, and vitamins.
APPLES & NUT BUTTER	A small sliced apple goes great with a tsp. of nut butter. Creamy, sweet, and savory, it also has some health benefits.
DRIED COCONUT	Unsweetened coconut can satisfy sweet cravings, but it also has fiber and healthy fats.
SUN-DRIED TOMATOES	These chewy tomatoes pack a lot of minerals and vitamins. They're also high in fiber, but have some protein as well. The ones packed in oil carry unnecessary fat calories.

SUGGESTIONS:

- Sometimes you just need an extra snack.
- Be careful about the times you snack. A snack tides you over between meals, but should not be necessary between every meal. Drink water instead of snacking before bed.
- Watch portions. If a snack is too large, it's really an extra meal.

COOKING WHOLE GRAINS

COOKING YIELDS AND PREPARATION

GRAIN (1 CUP DRY MEASURE)	WATER	COOK TIME	YIELD
7 OR 9 GRAIN CRACKED CEREAL	2 cups	15-20 minutes	2 ½ cups
BARLEY, PEARL	3 cups	25 minutes	3 ½ cups
BARLEY, HULLED	3 cups	45 minutes	3 cups
BUCKWHEAT	2 cups	15-20 minutes	2 ½ cups
BULGUR WHEAT	2 cups	15-20 minutes	2 ½ cups
CORNMEAL/POLENTA	4 cups	25 minutes	3 cups
CRACKED WHEAT	2 cups	25 minutes	2 ½ cups
MILLET	4 cups	45-60 minutes	4 cups
OAT GROATS	2 cups	15-20 minutes	2 ½ cups
OATS, WHOLE	2 cups	15-20 minutes	2 ½ cups
OATMEAL OR 5-GRAIN FLAKES	2 cups	10-20 minutes	2 ½ cups
RICE, BROWN	2 cups	60 minutes	3 cups
RICE, WILD	3 cups	60+ minutes	4 cups
RYE BERRIES	3 cups	60+ minutes	2 2/3 cups
WHEAT BERRIES	3 cups	60+ minutes	2 2/3 cups

STOVETOP DIRECTIONS:
1. Bring water to a boil in a heavy pot with a fitted lid, salting water if desired.
2. Stir in grain, cover, and reduce heat. Maintain a gentle simmer, but do not stir to avoid stickiness.
3. Grain is done when it is tender. If there is still water, uncover and simmer until evaporated.
4. Fluff with fork and serve.

HINT: For more flavor, you can roast whole grains before cooking by stirring continuously on med-high heat in a pan until golden brown (usually 3-5 minutes).

CROCKPOT DIRECTIONS:
1. Increase the cups of water and grain proportionately for larger batches.
2. Cook on low overnight.

MICROWAVE DIRECTIONS:
1. Place 1 cup of water, ½ cup cereal (oatmeal, 5-, 7-, or 9- grain flakes) and a pinch of salt in a large cereal bowl.
2. Cook on low power for 6 minutes. Stir when done. Add more time and liquid as necessary.
3. Add your favorite fruits, nuts, and toppings.

COOKING BEANS

COOKING YIELDS AND PREPARATION

BEANS (1 CUP DRY MEASURE)	WATER	COOK TIME	YIELD
ADZUKI BEANS	3 ½ cups	45-60 minutes	2 ½ cups
ANASAZI BEANS	2 cups	50-60 minutes	2 ½ cups
BLACK BEANS	3 cups	1 – 1 ½ hours	2 ½ cups
BLACK-EYED PEAS	3 ½ cups	1 – 1 ½ hours	2 ½ cups
GARBANZO BEANS (CHICKPEAS)	4-5 cups	4 – 5 hours	2 ½ cups
GREAT NORTHERN BEANS	3 ½ cups	1 ½ – 2 hours	2 ½ cups
KIDNEY BEANS	2 ½ cups	1 ½ – 2 hours	2 ½ cups
LENTILS, BROWN	3 cups	35-45 minutes	2 ½ cups
LENTILS, RED	3 cups	20-30 minutes	2 ½ cups
LIMA BEANS	3 ½ cups	1 ½ hours	2 ½ cups
MUNG BEANS	2 ½ cups	45-60 minutes	2 ½ cups
NAVY BEANS	3 cups	1 – 1 ½ hours	2 ½ cups
PINTO BEANS	3 cups	1 ½ – 2 hours	2 ½ cups
SOY BEANS	4 cups	3-4 hours	2 ½ cups
SPLIT PEAS	3 cups	45-60 minutes	2 ½ cups

STOVETOP DIRECTIONS:
1. Wash dry beans first and place in pot with water according to directions.
2. Bring to a boil.
3. Reduce heat, cover, and simmer until beans are tender but firm.

CROCKPOT DIRECTIONS:
1. Wash dry beans first and place in crockpot with water.
2. Add vegetables if desired, and cook overnight on high.

SUGGESTIONS FOR IMPROVING THE DIGESTION OF BEANS:
- Wash and soak beans for 8 hours. Rinse. Then cook as directed.
- Freeze beans prior to cooking. Follow directions after thawing. Place frozen beans in the pot. Boil uncovered for 10 minutes. Drain water. Add new water and cook beans until done.
- Cook beans with ginger or fennel.
- Make sure beans are cooked until tender. Hard beans can be more difficult to digest.

VEGAN SUBSTITUTIONS

MODIFY YOUR FAVORITE RECIPES WITH THESE INGREDIENTS

INGREDIENT	SUBSTITUTE
BUTTER	Use dairy-free, non-hydrogenated margarine for cooking, baking, or spreading.
CHEESE	Try vegan cheeses that use soy, rice, or nut-bases instead of dairy.
CREAM	Use soy-based cream, sour cream, or soy creamer. Pureed tofu, mashed potato, or nut milks may also work.
EGGS	<ul><li>¼ cup blended silken tofu</li><li>½ mashed medium banana</li><li>½ cup soy or rice yogurt</li><li>1 tbsp. ground flaxseed meal + 3 tbsp. water</li><li>¼ cup cooked oats</li><li>¼ cup mashed potato</li></ul>
MEAT	<ul><li>Beans</li><li>Mushrooms, especially Portobello</li><li>Seitan</li><li>Tempeh</li><li>Textured vegetable protein</li><li>Tofu</li><li>Veggie burgers</li></ul>
MILK	You can use almond, rice, soy, or other milk substitutes on a 1:1 ratio.
OIL	<ul><li>Substitute applesauce on a 1:1 ratio for oil when baking.</li><li>When sautéing, use water or vegetable broth.</li></ul>
PARMESAN	Check out our **Parmesan Cheese Substitute** Recipe.

SUGGESTIONS:

- Try to choose a substitute that will best fit the flavor profile of your recipe.
- In some cases, using too thick or too thin of a substitute may throw off your end result. Using a little extra water can help you if your recipe is looking too lumpy or thick. Thickeners, such as corn starch or other starches can be used in cases where things are too thin.

COOKING MEASUREMENTS

EASY REFERENCE CHART

MEASURE	EQUIVALENT
1 TBSP	3 tsp.
1/16 CUP	1 tbsp.
1/8 CUP	2 tbsp.
1/6 CUP	2 tbsp. + 2 tsp.
1/4 CUP	4 tbsp.
1/3 CUP	5 tbsp. + 1 tsp.
1/2 CUP	8 tbsp.
2/3 CUP	10 tbsp. + 2 tsp.
3/4 CUP	12 tbsp.
1 CUP	16 tbsp. or 8 oz.
1 PINT	2 cups or 16 oz.
1 QUART	4 cups, 2 pints, or 32 oz.
1 GALLON	4 quarts, 8 pints, 16 cups, or 128 oz.

SUGGESTIONS:

- It's often good to have 2 sets of measuring cups, in case you need one for wet and one for dry ingredients.
- Also invest in a nice set of measuring spoons. Graduated or double-sided ones can be handy, but are not necessary. Clean between uses.

CHIPPIN' IT OFF

HEALTHY LIVING SONG

I'm drinkin' water, not wine.
Eatin' veggies from the salad bar line.
Yea, I'm chippin' it off one pound at a time.
I quit cookies and ice cream, too.
My cholesterol is 162.
Cause I'm chippin' it off one pound at a time.

CHORUS:
I'm tellin' myself, that I know I can do it.
With the good Lord's help I'm gonna go right through it.
My lifestyle's a little bit different.
But I'll be fine, so fine.
Cause I'm chippin' it off one pound at a time.

I walk to work or ride my bike.
I grab a backpack and go on a hike.
Cause I'm chippin' it off one pound at a time.
No snackin', I'm eatin' rice.
I'm sleepin' better when I turn off the lights.
Yeah, I'm chippin' it off one pound at a time.

CHORUS:
I'm tellin' myself, that I know I can do it.
With the good Lord's help I'm gonna go right through it.
My lifestyle's a little bit different.
But I'll be fine, so fine.
Cause I'm chippin' it off one pound at a time.

Hey, I know I can do it.
With the good Lord's help I'm gonna go right through it.
My lifestyle's a little bit different.
But I'll be fine, so fine.
Cause I'm chippin' it off one pound at a time.

Yeah, I'm chippin' it off one pound at a time.
Who-oo-oo-oo
I'm healthy by choice, not chance.

Written by Woody Wright

HEALTHY LIVING AFFIRMATIONS

HEALTHY LIVING CHOICES

1. I am taking responsibility for my own health.
2. I plan ahead, because failing to plan is planning to fail.
3. Good health is a continuous choice I make every day.
4. I drink half of my weight in ounces of water every day.
5. I am committed to daily exercise.
6. I choose to eat a diet rich in whole grains.
7. I love to eat foods as grown.
8. I eat beans every day.
9. I limit my salt consumption.
10. I spend time in the sunshine and fresh air every day.
11. In my weakness, God can be strong.
12. I am healthy by choice, not by chance.

DESIGN & LAYOUTS BY:

WWW.MEDIASTREAMPRESS.COM

28318448R00046

Made in the USA
Columbia, SC
08 October 2018